ARRAN TO CANADA

- ONE WAY

James Henderson

ISBN 978-0-9564474-1-8

The contents of this book first appeared in Voice for Arran, though they have been re-edited to form a single story.

www.voiceforarran.com

Published by Voice for Arran online.

The Shire of BUTE
contains
BUTE and ARRAN.
with CANTIRE which is
Part of Argyle Shire 1725
By H. Moll Geographer.
The Cock of Arran
Rothesay
Clyd R.
Brodich or
Brodwick Castle
THE
Lambach or Holy
Island and Bay
ARRAN
FRITH OF
CLYD
Knockacharbit
Dounen
The Score of Pladda
Pladda I.
The Race of Pladda
Bennen Head
W. Bennen
E. Bennen
Myl of Torlean
Here is Plenty of Cod & Ling
Ailza

People and land

As the memorial in Lamlash reminds us, many people left Arran in the early nineteenth century to face an unknown future on the far side of the Atlantic Ocean. Trying to trace who they were and what happened to them makes it clear that their story is bound up with changes that broke up their traditional way of life in a move towards intensive agriculture. It was a massive shift, ruthlessly carried out, but the reasons for it were complex. The motive behind the Clearances that drove so many people out of Scotland was basically the desire of the landlords to make larger profits from farming, but on Arran, there was something more. People left because the whole pattern of their lives, together with their independence and self-respect, had been destroyed.

The imprint of that pattern is still with us, for there are countless places on the island where traces of the old run-rig system can be seen. The marks of the 'rigs' or long beds of ground show up clearly on the hillsides, especially in the spring, before bracken and rhododendron grow up to hide them. Slanting sunshine shows the dark and light striping of parallel ridges very clearly, running sideways across the hill to conserve moisture and prevent erosion.

The way these rigs were used is less well known. We visualise men and women – children, too – engaged in the hard labour of 'primitive' farming, but do not always realise how communal and effective the run-rig system was. All the people in the group co-operated to farm every plot, moving from one holding to the next as they carried out the necessary work of the season, regardless of who held the nominal tenancy. Working together brought a shared benefit, because every essential task was done quickly and thoroughly, at the right time, by a work-group big enough to complete it in no more than a day or two. It was far more efficient than having each plot farmed only by a single family, who would struggle with the long job of completing seasonal tasks unaided. Communal husbandry ensured that every tract of land was intensively cared for and productive.

On Arran, the run-rig system of mutual help had been established in the early ages, long before Scotland's ruling families declared themselves the owners of the land. Life in the small clachans was self-sufficient, as the rigs yielded enough to feed a family through the year, even though there were lean times. Money did not come into the picture. Peat dug from the hill and spread to dry on the heather provided heating, and clothes were made from hand-spun wool and flax. There were no shops and nothing to sell or buy. When the pattern of large-scale ownership came in, people had to find enough money to pay the annual rent. By the 18th century, when sporadic contact with the mainland began, this cost could be met by exporting any surplus produce that could be spared from essential use. Even so, farming was not a business, but a day-to-day means of survival.

In the economic difficulties of our own time, there is a growing respect for the idea of self-sufficiency and the independence it brings. 'Good life' settlers make a conscious effort to rediscover traditional skills, recognising that the global structure of imported goods may not be as permanent as we have been led to think. As oil supplies dwindle, the idea of sharing work to grow what we can may start to make sense all over again.

Arran's land-holdings had originally been hereditary, held for one or two-year periods and passed from father to son, with a rent permanently fixed by the overall landlord. The rent bought the right to farm, but communality demanded that everyone had an equal chance of farming the best land, so the rigs were allocated on a lottery system. The head man of each group, called in Gaelic the *fear a bhaile,* would gather the tenants together then each picked a single straw from the closed fistful he offered them. The man who picked the longest straw had his choice of the best land, followed by the others in order – a process that has left the phrase 'Picked the short straw' to describe anyone out of luck. The random selection was designed to give everyone an equal chance to farm the best or worst ground, but since all of it was worked communally, nobody had to struggle alone.

The Dukes of Hamilton, who had ruled Arran except for a brief period when the Covenanters and the Campbells took over, had for many years been content to allocate the blocks of rigs for each clachan and leave the *fear a bhaile* to conduct the traditional distribution of plots. They took a small rent, but regarded the system as a settled way of life rather than a business. From their point of view, the strength and ability of the people was a valuable asset, for part of the understanding was that all island men would fight on the Duke's side if there should there be an invasion or uprising. Arran's men and women lived what would now be seen as an ideally healthy life, eating nothing but fresh, home-grown food and depending entirely on their own physical fitness to continue a life that demanded unremitting work. They had for hundreds of years been a hardy race, well able to come to the defence of the island if necessary, and the ruling Dukes were happy to allow them to fish and take an occasional pheasant or grouse. It was a small concession to set against the knowledge that an effective scratch army was always at hand, should it be needed.

OLD NICOL STREET, LAMLASH

For Arran people, the way of life was settled. Though it required constant physical work, the only major risk lay in the weather. For most of the year, there was no surplus to sell, but the annual rent fell due at Michaelmas, which was the easiest time of the year. Salted butter, made by the girls and women who lived up the hill with the cattle during the summer months, kept well and found ready sales on the mainland. Michaelmas was also the traditional killing time, and dried meat, too, could be exported.

Fish abounded in the sea, but catching them was a difficult and dangerous art. Making and mending nets and building and repairing small boats took a lot of work, but fish formed an important part of the diet. Again, it was not a commercial activity. A bounty was paid to mainlanders who owned relatively large boats and brought in a big catch for sale, but inshore fishermen were not eligible for this.

In the main, people ate what could be grown. The run-rig system produced oats, barley, peas and beans, with a crop of hay in the summer when the cattle were turned out on the hill. Green vegetables had not at that time been introduced, though the exceptionally hardy kale was a good food for both animals and humans. Butter, cheese and the occasional rabbit, game bird or deer provided fats and protein, and dried meat lasted for some time in the winter. Potatoes became an important crop later, but also brought disaster when the appalling disease of potato blight caused devastation.

Cereals were important. Oats grew well in hard conditions and were a staple food, useful both for humans and animals. Bere was a form of barley probably brought to Britain by Vikings in the 9th century. It grew very fast and was well suited to soils of a low pH value. It used to be known as 'the 90-day barley', quickly providing grain for milling and malting as well as straw for thatching and animal bedding.

A three-plot system of rotation ensured that land remained fertile. A crop was produced in the first year, and for the second, the plot was left fallow. On the third, it was used for grazing, and benefited from the dung of the animals. Seaweed was collected from the shore, at specified places agreed by the landlord, and acted as a good fertiliser – as it still does for canny Arran farmers whose land runs down to a beach.

There were no villages on Arran in the early 18th century. Brodick, Lamlash, Whiting Bay and the rest grew up in the Victorian age, as can be seen from the style of their buildings. Maps from the earlier period show small groups of black-houses and barns surrounded by the allocated rigs. There was little farming in the north of the island, where granite predominates and topsoil is scant, but it was close-packed wherever the land was fertile. One clachan beside another filled the edge of the island in a continuous run from Sannox all the way round the South end, interrupted only where cliffs rise straight from the sea. Settlements also followed river glens up the hills as far as possible, though they petered out where arable land gave way to moor. The furthest inland were Kilmichael, 'Monnyquill' above Machrie and Glen Scoredale, as it was then spelled.

Arran's population was counted in the 1750s as 3646, and it was self-sufficient. A packet-boat came over from Saltcoats once a week, but people grew their own food, butchered their own meat and made their own clothes. One of the island's attractions for visitors was the goats' milk being produced at Cladach, for this was supposed to be good for the health. Roads barely existed, and anything too heavy for a man to lift was hauled on a rough sledge that could slide over heather or stony land. Life was hard and relentlessly busy, but it was sustainable. The changes that lay ahead could not at that time have been imagined.

Ambition

The Union of 1707 had brought the Scottish aristocracy, whose members almost without exception owned the land let out to small tenants, into close contact with the Westminster government. They were frequently in London, hobnobbing (or arguing) with English colleagues, and they were no doubt anxious to be seen as forward-looking and capable. They had endured considerable scorn from their English colleagues in the House of Commons, who were quick to mock the accent of any Scot brave enough to venture an opinion. Sir John Clerk had roared at the English members to mind their manners after receiving a snide comment for pronouncing 'water' as 'watter', but despite such courage, the Scots must have smarted at the idea that these sophisticated Southerners found them laughable. Given the choice of changing the old ways or defending them, change was by far the preferable option.

Scotland had lost half its male population and much of its total financial resource in the Darien disaster, an effort to found a trading colony in Panama that failed catastrophically. Malaria and other tropical diseases had decimated the hopeful Scots, and the English settlers, when appealed to for help in repelling Spanish attacks, flatly refused. The disaster had sharpened Scotland's financial need to accept the Union, while England, conversely, was riding high. It had seen an end to the protracted Civil War and the Duke of Hamilton had solved 'the Scottish problem' when he proposed that Scottish MPs should be appointed directly by the Queen. The London government could now rest assured that there would be no more trouble with their northern neighbours, and the main task ahead was to make money. Wealthy merchants were returning from the Indies, and trade was flourishing. The price of land – and almost everything else – was rising fast.

The English had been quick to perceive that agriculture could be a rich source of profit. New and more powerful fertilisers were becoming available from previously undiscovered countries such as Chile, and much research was being done on new and more intensive farming methods. The Scottish lords were quick to see that these discoveries could be exploited to their own advantage. They saw, too, that in order to benefit from this modernity, the run-rig system and the tenants who depended on it would have to be swept away.

The people of Arran would not have known about this intention. The Lairds lived in a different world of money and business and travel, and besides, London was a long way from Scotland. News travelled slowly, if at all, and those in power had nothing to gain from warning the tenants what was in store for them. Peaceful Scottish people such as the Arran islanders, who had had taken no active part in the rising of 1745, would not have realised how unpopular the dissident Highlanders were among supporters of the Union. The Forty-Five, described by Robert McLellan in his book, *The Isle of Arran* as 'the last fling of the Gaels against the forces threatening their language, costume, customs and economy' had greatly annoyed and embarrassed the London-based Scottish aristocracy. They were only too ready to share the English view of all Highland people (including islanders) as an unruly rabble that needed to be brought to heel. The climate of opinion among the aristocracy was firmly against run-rig tenants, and there would be little sympathy for those who found themselves discarded in the movement towards improvement and profit.

Arran's landowner of the time, James, sixth Duke of Hamilton, had been in Paris at the time of the Forty-Five, but on return to London, he accepted the new idea of profitable agriculture with alacrity. He gave his instructions about how Arran should be improved, but by 1766 he had died. The title passed to his son, but the boy died of a fever not long afterwards, so his younger brother, Douglas Douglas-Hamilton, became the eighth Duke. Douglas, born at the Palace of Holyroodhouse in 1756, was only ten years old, and was being educated at Eton. He had little to do with Arran - in fact, there is no evidence that he ever set foot on the island - but curiously, he later married Elizabeth Anne Burrell. Whether she was related to the John Burrell who was to bring such vast changes to Arran must remain speculative, but the young duke's mother detested the match, saying that 'the daughter of a private gentleman, however accomplished', was 'not qualified to be allied' to any son of hers. The couple stayed together until 1794 but had no children and eventually divorced by Act of Parliament.

In 1746, what the ruling family was doing hardly mattered. The old duke's trustees had been well briefed, and needed no encouragement to carry forward his plans. They had seen the profits being made from 'improved' agriculture and were in full agreement that Arran's farming methods must be modernised. Lord Eglinton, whose English servants had already introduced seed-drilling and the culture of turnips into Ayrshire, was achieving good results. The price of agricultural produce was galloping upwards. Corn was fetching at least one-third more, and cattle were changing hands at double the price ever seen in the previous thirty years. The time was ripe to bring Arran into this newly promising state.

In 1766, as luck for the land-owner had it, many of the leases on Arran's larger Arran farms were running out.

These lands had traditionally been let for periods of nineteen years, for which the tenants had paid a one-off 'grassum', but all that was set to change. The young Duke's advisers wasted no more time. They needed an experienced, thick-skinned man to get the improvements started, and to shoulder the blame for any discomfort it might cause. They appointed Mr. John Burrell, their factor at Kinneil, and gave him a free hand to reorganise Arran's farming methods.

Patrick Murray, writing in 1910, had done some extensive research on Arran's history, and he was no great admirer of Burrell. He said, 'This man ... was, judging by name, probably English or of English origin. He was a perfect stranger, at any rate, and there is no one like a stranger for the work if you want the old landmarks removed, for a stranger knows no traditions, feels no sentimental scruples.'

Burrell visited Arran at least nine times from 1766 to 1782, for periods ranging from one to four months. Lady Jean Fforde had two of his diaries privately published, producing 150 copies of the hand-written entries for 1766-73 and

1776-82. It is a massive volume, measuring 17 X 11 inches (43X28 cm), written in a sloping copperplate with ornate double-sized headings for the details of each farm. Deciphering it is not easy. Much of it is a detailed survey of every holding on the island, together with stock held, crops grown and an assessment of the quality of the land, but personal touches creep in, some of which raise a wry smile.

Crossing to Arran from the mainland, then as now, could be problematic. Burrell was stormbound at Saltcoats for almost a week in September 1772, then was woken early one morning by Captain Bannatyne, who said the weather had improved and they would attempt a sailing. Several passengers boarded the wherry, a timber-built sailing craft with four oars, and they left Saltcoats at 6am. However, the wind changed direction and by the time they reached Arran, the waves were so tempestuous that they could not land. At mid-day they headed for the sheltered side of Holy Isle and discharged the passengers to wait until a local boat could take them over to Lamlash when the weather improved. It's a tale to bear in mind when CalMac is having a minor hiccup.

Burrell's 'strict survey', as he called it, was in the service of a very definite aim. He had been commissioned to undertake the task of turning Arran's agriculture into a profitable business, and the most urgent prerequisite for this, in his view, was the dismantling of the run-rig system. Communal work would be ended. Instead, the land would be parcelled into much larger enclosures, so that the old holdings would be grouped together within a single wall or hedge as big, efficient farms. The young Duke was much taken with this proposal and was happy to spend large sums on the work Burrell suggested. An overseer and a gang of workmen were brought from the mainland to build dykes round several newly-enclosed farms as an example of what was wanted, following which, the new tenants themselves were expected to continue the work. Forty spades were ordered from Ayrshire to begin with, then Arran smiths were encouraged to make more.

Where stone was not available or people would not co-operate, the dykes were simply made of turf. These can still be seen in many places on Arran. Those at Drumadoon, Blairbeg, Torbeg and Tormore were some of the first made, to Burrell's orders. Meanwhile, animals were not to be turned loose to graze in the traditional way. Where enclosed fields had not been established, they were to be tethered and moved as necessary. In mainland Ayrshire the Levellers destroyed such enclosures in furious night-time forays, but their protest was soon stamped out.

On Arran, people perhaps did not at first realise the magnitude of the change that was set to overwhelm them. Some were immediately dispossessed, but others tried to work within the new system – and were dismayed to find that the re-set tacks, or lease prices, were far higher than ever before. Burrell was impervious to all protest. His remit was to encourage new and profitable farming, and he saw the old run-rig system as the main impediment to this. He hated the concept of communal work and called it 'barbarous'.

The fact that there would be no provision for run-rig tenants who lost their homes and their means of survival did not appear to concern him. He was more interested in ensuring that the tenants of the larger, enclosed farms conducted their business profitably. He complained that the small farmers had far too many horses, and tried to persuade them to use draught oxen instead. The old-established Arran farming families had always enjoyed certain long-established rights, but Burrell abolished these, setting the old families on the same level as any newcomer and causing grievous resentment. He made it clear that his main interest was in profitable enterprise, no matter of what kind. He opened a lime quarry in the Clachan Glen and a slate quarry at Lochranza. He ordered an exploratory dig for coal at the Cock Farm, and put down a bore at Clauchlands. These things did nothing to reassure Arran people, who watched in dismay as everything they had known was undone. In that pivotal year of 1766, every farm and holding on the island had its tenancy suspended so that the new system could begin.

It did not happen without protest. The tenants, shocked by the hike in their annual rent, argued with good reason that they had no money to meet the steep increases. Burrell clearly took this to be proof of the inefficiency of the old system, based as it was on subsistence farming that kept families fed but produced little that could be sold - and so he and the tenants were deadlocked in opposition.

Time and again, the diary records Burrell's frustration at arriving at a pre-agreed meeting with tenants only to find that they did not turn up. On March 15th 1770, he wrote, 'We sate the whole Day with patience, and altho all the [various villages] tennants should have this day appeared, with their Rent, none of them came.' By April 6th, his exasperation boiled over. Infuriated by the 'audacity, impudence and chicanery of these fellows', he threatened them with 'Total Ejection ... after which they were glad to sign.'

Continued resistance, and the sheer impossibility of getting more than a certain amount of blood out of a stone wore

Burrell down, however, and by the end of that year he had settled for haggling rather than complete intransigence. Bargains, of a kind, were struck, and for those who could scrape together enough money, farming continued.

For the others, there was nothing.

Loss

Burrell had assumed that the communal system of run-rig cultivation reflected the stupidity of the people engaged in it. A later observer, Loudon, disagreed, and said it was 'Admirably suited to the circumstances in which it originated, the plan having been conceived in wisdom and executed with extraordinary accuracy.'

No such perception entered Burrell's thinking, and his journals make clear his low opinion of the island. He found the husbandry primitive and complained that the bridges were made of wood, the connection with the mainland was irregular and letters were delivered haphazardly 'as opportunity offered.' It irked him that the boat fare to Ayr was 15 shillings and the boats were badly constructed and 'deficient in the matter of tackle.' Worst, from his point of view, was that the whole of the island, save the park of Brodick Castle, was unenclosed, with no single person in charge of it. Since the people obstinately insisted on working freely for each other, no profit whatever was being made.

In a very few years, all that had changed – and as a result, people who had lost their homes and their livelihood were destitute. They started to constitute a problem, being unemployed and with no resources. Burrell regarded them as a nuisance, and when the first people started to emigrate from Scotland, he seized on it as an admirable solution.

As early as 1770, people had started to leave the island. The names of those first emigrants were not recorded. Nobody in authority was bothered about what happened to this human detritus left from the improvements – the main thing was to get rid of it. We have no record of what happened to that first ship-load of people who set out on the two months' voyage to America. Burrell's only comment was that it was dangerous to suspend the Baron Court for six months at that point, as had been planned. With so many people intending to go to America, he said, 'to leave the place ...without a judge would be leaving it in the power of these emigrants to rob both his grace and their neighbours.' Patrick Murray, a later writer, was appalled and said to suggest that heart-broken people 'would rob their own unfortunate kinsfolk' seemed 'wanton and without justification in fact or precedent.'

Burrell's journal notes that those in a state of 'hatred and despair' were plotting against the Duke, though there is no record of any actual rebellion. John Paterson, described by Murray as 'an able and not unkindly factor of the estate', reported in his 1837 Account of the Island of Arran that the people had 'opposed the changes in every way short of physical resistance', but they were in no position to consider out-and-out rebellion.

Paterson had some respect for Arran, and although he did his bit to suppress the use of the Gaelic language, he described the people as 'hospitable amongst themselves and to strangers,' and said he found them 'more confiding in each other than is altogether prudent.' He added, 'The money and other property of the more fortunate among them are freely lent to those in need, often when there is but a slight prospect of repayment. To their aged and infirm relations they are generally kind and dutiful, and scarcely any are ever allowed to beg their bread.' He went on to remark, 'The people of Arran may justly be described as a religious community ... so far as recollected, there is not a single native who can with justice be called a drunkard.' Ten years later, however, he wrote with concern about what had happened. 'A deep dejection appears in general through the countenances of all: no time can be spared for amusement of any kind, the whole being given for procuring the means of paying their rent, of laying in their fuel, or getting in a scanty pittance of meat and clothing.'

One of Burrell's first actions had been to form in 1770 an administrative committee. Its members were George Couper, William MacGregor, Patrick Hamilton, John Hamilton, Gershom Stewart (minister of Kilbride), Duncan Mac-Bride, John Pette, John Fullarton, Gavin Fullarton, John Hamilton, Thomas Brown, William Ogg, Hector MacAllister, Alexander MacGregor, John MacCook, and Adam Fullarton.

REMAINS OF THE RUNRIG SYSTEM

SHEEP AT NOTH GLEN SANNOX WITH THE REMAINS OF ONE OF THE OLD FARMS IN THE BACKGROUND.

Ten of these men were dependent on work provided by the Duke of Hamilton and so were bound to support Mr. Burrell's measures. Of the others, at least four were directly or indirectly employed by the Arran estate manager, so the committee could hardly be seen as democratic. Its intentions were essentially organisational, designed to further their own purposes. They wanted a service of packet boats running between the island and Saltcoats, but all other concerns centred on control and regulation of the new farming system.

The tenants were to keep herds and to fold their cattle every night, 'according to Act of Parliament.' Sheep were to be marked, and no cattle or sheep could be killed without calling together a jury of the three nearest neighbours. All weights and measures were to be taken to the castle, and compared with Ayr weights and measures.

Thomas Pennant (1726-1798), an Englishman whose *Tour of Scotland and Voyage in the Hebrides* contains interesting views, noted with concern that on Arran the farms were 'advanced by unnatural force to above double the old rent'. He had written in earlier days about the songs and story telling, the gaiety and the general colour by which life in the Highlands had been characterised, but in 1772 his observations were very different. He noted with regret the dejection of the people following the splitting up of the old, co-operative way of working, and said that in place of mutually agreed work, there was now quarrelling over the details of rights and ownership.

The increases continued to creep up over the years. In 1778, according to Burrell's own figures, the actual rent-total of the island was in round terms at least £5550. If additions from some tenants were counted in, it came to £5880. The pattern of tenancy changed into something very different.

It had been decided to divide the 99 run-rig farms on Arran, then supporting some 1100 families through the system of communal work, into 250 smaller farms, each of which would support just a single family. The first leases came up for renewal in 1772, but the process took much longer than Burrell had planned. It was not until 70 years later that the Duke of Hamilton's estate had finally been divided into 458 family farms. On the western side of the island, a dogged inertia persisted for two or three decades, and the new methods did not find acceptance until well into the nineteenth century.

By 1776, premiums were being offered in order to encourage good husbandry. They are well recorded. The tenant producing the best three-year-old 'humbled' bull of his own property, not under the value of £10 could win 5 guineas, and 2½ guineas would reward the tenant who produced 'the best two-year-old tup of Bakewell and Chaplin kind—full blood—not under the value of £5.' The best three-year-old entire horse, not under the value of £15 and not above 15 hands high stood to win 7½ guineas. The prizes were handsome, and laid the ground for what is now the annual Agricultural Show.

6 guineas rewarded the tenant with the best field of turnips, not under 3 acres, 'sown broad-cast after a summer fallow by 3 ploughings, and manured. And to him who shall have the best field not under 3 acres, in drills 2½ feet distance, horsehoed no less than 3 times, and the ground well manured—5 guineas.'

Cabbages were strongly encouraged, to be planted at 4 feet between rows, and 2 feet apart, but this crop was meant as stock feed. 20,000 plants (three times horsehoed) should, if the plants weighed 4 lbs each, fatten 16 head of cattle in 9 weeks.

Arable crops were not forgotten, either. 'To the tenant who shall have the greatest quantity and best quality of wheat upon enclosed ground, and after a thorough summer fallow of 5 furrows, sufficiently manured, and no less than 2 acres—2 guineas.' Clover and rye-grass hay were similarly rewarded, if 'properly manured, and not less than 100 stones an acre, and upon enclosed ground.'

Amongst the prize-winners in the two years following were Angus MacKillop, Alexander Thomson, Patrick Crawford, Robert Shaw, John Currie, and Alexander MacKinnon. There were many, however, who had no land and could enter no competitions. By about 1810, Murray wrote, 'The condition of all save the few big tacksmen was miserable ... their houses were the meanest hovels, while they were clad in the coarsest garments of home manufacture.' The difficulty of staying alive sapped all energy, and killed the hard-working cheerfulness and the enjoyment of music and fun that had once enlivened the community.

Hardship and potatoes

By 1880 the Hamilton Arran estate comprised 99 farms, supporting over 1,100 individuals but that was a century after the beginning of the improvements that changed life on the island forever. In the mid-1870s, many of the dispossessed people who had lost their traditionally shared land hated the new ideas and wanted nothing to do with them. Agricultural labouring for some larger farmer was very different from the self-employed, varied work that had been within every individual's own control. However, those who objected were on their own, with no resources. There were so many of these derelict people that employed workers were unlikely to complain. One farm in the South end of the island had a population of 300 souls (between 30 & 40 couples with their families), working as they were told, obedient to the new scheme.

Intensive production was the aim. One of the biggest changes was the introduction of fertiliser. Agricultural chemistry was a new science, unknown to the peasant farmers who had regarded seaweed and cattle dung as the natural enrichment of the soil. They had been happy to let the land rest and recover for a fallow year and never dreamed that it could be coaxed into far higher yields. Burrell had learned about the newly-available fertilisers discovered through exploration of other countries, and lost no time in making use of them. By the early 1800s, nitrogen fertiliser was being imported from Chile in the form of guano. Lime was brought to Arran by the Clyde 'puffers', which often beached on sandy areas where farmers could load the cargo onto carts at low tide. Sulphate of ammonia and super phosphate started to be manufactured, and these enriched vegetables and root crops that had come into increased use when bread became very expensive.

To handle this increased production, mechanisation came into use. Reaping and threshing machines were a new sight on Arran and metal ploughs and drills replaced the old wooden tools. Larger, heavier carts were needed, and so were roads for them to use. As motorists have been ruefully aware to this day, Arran's roads came from cart tracks and were never built with the engineering skills that the Romans

GATHERING PEAT

had understood. Before the 1800s, people used wooden sledges to move things across rough ground and heather-covered moors. All this was set to change. With Government assistance, the landowner paid for a road between Brodick and Gorton Alister, Lamlash, and people realised the blessing of being able to use wheeled carts on a relatively smooth surface.

Working with iron became newly vital as horses treading the hard surfaces of the new roads had to be shod and cartwheels needed to be iron-rimmed. Almost every community had its own blacksmith, as can be seen from the various 'smiddy' references still found on the island. Lamlash had two smithies, one in the area of the present Aldersyde, the other opposite Glencraig. The local blacksmith had many uses, not all of them agricultural. He sometimes acted as a desperate port of call for locals suffering from toothache.

Arran, though an island, has never been unaffected by national legislation, and its agriculture was increasingly influenced by wider circumstances. The Corn Laws

THE SMIDDY AT THE ARRAN HERITAGE MUSEUM AS IT WAS IN THE 1800'S

introduced at the beginning of the 19th century to protect British farmers had resulted in a huge rise in the price of wheat, and this had brought tragedy to Ireland. There, the appallingly badly treated tenant farmers saw the corn they had grown loaded onto ships bound for the rich markets of England, while they and their families were starving. The same ruthless profiteering was happening in the Scottish Highlands and islands, but with the vital difference that the people were not so dependent on wheat, since it is not a good crop for hill farms. The traditional diet was based on oats, and this was not too badly affected. Ireland, with no such alternative resource, turned in desperation to the potato, a vegetable introduced for the tables of the gentry but cheap and easy to grow.

Potatoes were relatively new to the European farming scene. They had been discovered in Central America, where they had been used extensively since pre-Columbian times, and explorers were quick to realise that this was a valuable, highly nutritious crop. It was easy to grow, and could yield a very profitable harvest.

HARVESTING AT CORRIEGILLS, ISLE OF ARRAN

When potatoes first came to Britian in the mid-1700s, they were regarded with deep suspicion, since they were known to belong to the poisonous nightshade family. However, their usefulness was soon obvious. In about 1780, when Ireland was struggling to survive the punitive effect of the Corn Laws, the arrival of the potato came as a miracle. It was a source of abundant, nutritious food, and it soon became the staple diet. But it carried a hidden danger that nobody suspected.

The potato blight Phytophthura Infestans is an air-borne fungus that causes the tubers to turn into a mushy mess, completely inedible. It first began in a mountain range of Mexico and destroyed crops in America, then migrated across the Atlantic in infected ships and appeared in France. From there it came to the Isle of Wight, then arrived in Ireland. In 1845, ideal weather conditions had raised expectations of a bumper harvest, but the disease wiped out the entire crop. It left no seed stock for the following season, and in any case, the ground was hopeless polluted by the fungus. The blight raged unstoppably for a further 3-4 years, and over a quarter of Ireland's population died of starvation.

Carried by the prevailing westerly wind, the disease migrated to Scotland in the following year, 1846. Arran, in common with all the Highlands and islands, was hit by it. However, the island farmers, being less constrained by need than their Irish counterparts, returned instinctively to crop rotation, resting the afflicted ground and diversifying into other crops. They realised, too, that the best fields for potato growing were the ones adjacent to the shore, fertilised by the traditional seaweed. James Allan cautiously purchased two bags of Champion seed potatoes, and they returned a good crop and became very popular all over the Island.

Experimenting with varieties of potato that might prove blight-immune worked triumphantly well. In 1879 the potato crop at the Clauchlands farm yielded 12 to 15 tons per acre, setting records for high production. The potato crop was stored in pits for later sale, and secured prices of £3.00 to £5.00 per ton. Confidence returned, and farmers planted a wide range of varieties, including Walkers Early, Red Bogs, Regents, Dalmahoys, Skerry Blues and the Champion. The famous Arran potato breeds came later, in the early 1900s, developed by Donald MacKelvie. A horticulturalist rather than a farmer, he had been born in Lamlash on the 24th February 1867, but spent most of his youth in Dennistoun in Glasgow, where he studied accountancy. He returned to Lamlash at the age of 24 and assisted his Aunt Jessie McNeish in the family bakery, which is now the Lamlash Co-op. His interest in potatoes began with a friend's gift of a new variety, and he cultivated these experimental strains in the fields surrounding the site of the present High School. There can be few people who do not know of the Arran Pilot or of course of the Arran Banner, but there were other varieties as well, including the Arran Victory and the Arran Consul. MacKelvie was honoured for his work in February 1925, at a dinner in the Douglas Hotel attended by farmers and business men from all parts of Britain. He was awarded the OBE in 1945, and died at at the age of 80 at his home in Lamlash, a house named New Lanark.

Such development of the potato was unknown in the mid-1800s, and the famine and suffering ran unchecked. The Corn Laws were repealed as a result of international outrage over the British government's indifference to Ireland's plight. Irish-grown wheat had made high profits for the men who exported it, while the farmers who had grown the corn saw their children dying of hunger. Farmers learned a bitter new lesson – that when cultivation of the land turns into agri-business, the international market controls both the product and its producer.

LAMLASH - THESE COTTAGES WERE REMOVED TO BUILD HAMILTON TERRACE

SANDBRAES, WHITING BAY

Smuggling

Home-produced whisky had always cheered the mind and brought comfort to cold bones, and many people in the blackhouses up the hill used some of the barley they grew for a little quiet distilling. In the early 1800s the landowners neither knew nor cared what the tenant farmers got up to, as long they paid their rents. If they made the necessary money through the output of a small pot-still, it was no cause for outrage. The exciseman whom Burns wished awa' with the Deil did not get going until the mid-eighteenth century, when whisky was realised to be a highly profitable product, far too valuable to be in the hands of ignorant peasants. Like the land itself, it was argued, such a resource should be enclosed for the use of the wealthy and the properly competent. But the small distilling that went on in the clachans was not easy to root out.

Bere, the hardy traditional barley that stood up well to Arran's often blustery weather, had always made a good whisky. It was probably largely ignored in the push towards heavier-yielding crops, but it could easily be grown in any odd corner, and it was used extensively in Arran's illegal distilling.

The taxation of whisky drove a powerful wedge between the recognised commercial distillers and the secret production that continued in the clachans. What had been as natural a part of small farming as baking or brewing became a far more attractive enterprise, since cheap, untaxed whisky found ready buyers. Smuggling home-produced hooch turned into something between a business and a sport, offering both profit and danger. Patrick Murray, who was sentimentally inclined to see the Arran people as 'pre-eminently law-abiding', made excuses for them. He said they must have assumed that the product of their stills was 'so very good that they could not find it in their hearts to believe that any law could make the making of it bad.'

This may have been a trifle naïve. Smuggling of the famous 'Arran water' became a major activity, continued in the teeth of all opposition. Murray states that there were 32 illicit stills in Arran in 1784. Of these, 23 were in the south end – a fact that will surprise nobody living on Arran today. The introduction of Malt Duty established the Revenue men as the Islanders' enemy, and they patrolled the island frequently in their cutter, the *Prince Edward*, a fast two-masted sloop. Successful arrests led to heavy fines, and a father, son and daughter who were cited to appear at court in Rothesay were fined the large sum of sixty pounds – an indication of the money to be made from distilling. Despite such penalties, smuggling continued well into the nineteenth century, and sometimes led to tragedy.

On March 27th 1817 a boat sailed from Arran's south end with a load of illicit whisky, but changed course sharply on catching sight of the revenue cutter. The revenue officers spotted the sudden switch of direction and launched their small liberty boat with a crew of 10 men. It was faster than the heavily laden Arran boat, and quickly overtook the smugglers, forcing them to land on the island. There, the excisemen seized the contraband whisky and started to take the illicit barrels back to the cutter. Local people, aware of what was going on, tried to come to the rescue, but it led to disaster. Two Arran men and one woman were shot dead in the ensuing fight, and two children were wounded. The men were both McKinnons, father and son, and the woman was Isabel Nichol. A court case held in Rothesay on September 9th the same year found that John Jeffrey, the mate of the *Prince Edward* revenue cutter, was not guilty of murder. The jury agreed with the defendant's lawyer, who held that Jeffrey was defending his men in pursuance of their duty.

The incident must have been a sobering one, in every sense, for Arran people, but the final blow to home distilling came when a further Act of Parliament stipulated that small stills in the Highlands of Scotland must be licensed. Anyone found to be in possession of an unlicensed still was liable, along with his tenants, for a heavy fine. This put pressure on the landowner and on the legal distillers, who took fright at the idea that they would be held responsible for what their tenants got up to. They caved in and brought pressure to bear on their small lease-holders, many of whom were forced to give up. After the passing of the Act, 26 stills were collected and carried to the Castle.

It was perhaps not such a large proportion as it sounds. Murray quotes a letter written in 1797 that assumed there were no fewer than 50 stills in the south end of the island. At that time the whole annual output of Arran's bere was being used for distilling. The practice survived throughout the eighteenth century, but in the early nineteenth, the Duke of Hamilton took a strong line, and threatened to dispossess any tenant convicted of illicit distillation. That was the final blow. Illegal distilling decreased and at last disappeared entirely, as far as can be seen. However, people alive today who walked the Highlands a mere fifty years ago will tell you of meeting people cheerfully drunk on some high moor, though all the local hotels claimed to be strictly Temperance.

Traces of the old activity still remain on Arran. The ruins of a malt kiln stood for a long time in the grounds of the Whitehouse, in Lamlash, and may still be there under the brambles. It had been a licensed still with a capacity of forty gallons, from which, in the single year of December 1793 to November 1794, whisky was sold to the amount of £500 – a prodigious sum in those days. The precious liquid cost two shillings (ten pence) a pint, but was cheaper in bulk, at four shillings (twenty pence) a gallon. At eight pints to the gallon, it was a bargain.

The island's ministers were righteously shocked by the smuggling – though some were more shocked than others. The Rev. J. Kennedy Cameron sounds tight-lipped in his memoir of the Rev. John MacAlister, observing that, 'Smuggling was common in Arran at that time, and John MacAlister took his share in smuggling adventures like the rest.' Paterson, writing in 1830, strongly denied that Arran was a drunken island and pointed out that a religious revival had arisen in Kilmory, led by the Rev. Neil MacBride.

Arran was not the only place in which there was smuggling. It was carried out on every coast of Scotland, including Burrell's own neighbourhood of the Forth, bordering the respectable city of Edinburgh. It is only in very recent years that travellers returning from abroad have not had to open cases for a Customs inspection. Something of the smuggler perhaps lurks in us all.

The haves and the have-nots

The big changes that had come about had driven a wedge between the favoured and the others. Those who had agreed (and could afford) to be a part of the enclosed and more profitable system had lost the old communality, but as individuals, most of them prospered.

The invention of the metal plough, as opposed to the lighter one made of wood, meant more strength was needed to pull it. Burrell's favouring of oxen as draught animals had failed to wean islanders from their traditional love of horses. The powerful Shire horse was introduced to Arran, and breeding of the hardy Highland pony was stepped up. By 1880 the Highland Agriculture Society of Scotland noted that most farms now had their own horse. On Arran, a few reared the famous 'Douglas', augmenting their meagre income by hiring out this smart trotter, harnessed to a buggy for tourists to drive. Including horses, cattle and sheep, livestock increased by 3,000 head. The local cow breed was unique to Arran, evolved from Ayrshire, West Highlander, Arran and Irish stock.

Arran's geology makes the north of the island unsuitable for arable farming, consisting mostly of granite sand, and the areas of good loam are limited to the gentler land in the south. When the old run-rig system ended, only six of the new farms were big enough to incur a rent of £100 a year or more. Eleven paid between £40-£100, thirty paid less than £40, but the vast majority paid only £20.

A man writing in 1880 looked back without great regret to the days when working the fields was a family affair, with the man controlling the plough handles, women leading the ponies and children driving them, and spoke of 'the improved wage structure of the farms.' By then, dairymaids were receiving between £8.00 and £12.00 for 6 months, with board. Ploughmen were paid £12 to £15.00 for 6 months with board, but they were often expected to work 10 to 12 hour days, six days a week, starting from 6.00 a.m. At harvest time casual labourers (some men but mainly women) received 2 shillings and sixpence to four shillings per day, but had to bring their own food. During the planting of potatoes or for turnip thinning the same workers received one shilling to one shilling and sixpence per day.

Shepherds were engaged on an annual basis of £40.00. In addition, they had a free house, an allowance for coal or supply of peat, grazing for up to 2 cows and an area planted with potatoes – which goes to show how highly valued sheep had become. By the standards of the time, the wages were good, considering that in 1915, more than a hundred years later, a nurse (female, of course) was paid £4 a year plus her keep. On Arran, those in the system were doing well.

In 1817 the String road was built, connecting Brodick and Shiskine, then the Ross, to link Lamlash and the South End. Another new road linked Brodick and Sannox. Better sea connections were established, too, when the steamboat *Helensburgh* began sailings from Greenock to Arran via Rothesay, returning via Millport. In 1860 a service run by the Ardrossan Steamboat Co linked Brodick and Lamlash to Ardrossan, using a steamer called the *Earl of Arran*. In 1868 the 12th Duke of Hamilton and the Arran Estate trustees moved into the transport business, running two vessels from Brodick, the *Lady Mary* and the *Heather Bell*, but six

THE PS IVANHOE AT THE FERRY ROCK CORRIE

years later, approached Captain Buchanan and asked him to take it over.

Piers were being constructed to serve the increased steamer traffic. The original Brodick Pier was built in 1871 of wrought iron, and was opened to the public the following year, on June 17th. Lamlash Pier followed in 1884 and Lochranza four years later in 1888. Whiting Bay got its pier in 1899.

The paddle steamers ran a daily service of one return journey and changed the lifestyle of the residents, enabling them to think about the mainland as reasonably accessible. Clyde paddle steamers called at Corrie, Brodick, Lamlash, Kings Cross and Whiting Bay on the island's east coast and Lochranza, Pirnmill, Machrie, and Blackwaterfoot on the West, en route to Campbeltown. Where there were no piers, small local rowing boats were used to ferry passengers and goods ashore.

Two years ago Lamlash pier was reopened after extensive repairs were made to modernise it, but this summer it will be closed once more and Brodick will take the major traffic for Arran. Changed days for Lamlash, once the most thriving port on the island. Here you see it in 1860, its safe harbour crowded with shipping and the paddle steamer, Earl of Arran, lying at the old stone pier.

The influx of holidaymakers began to have a big influence on Arran's appearance. New buildings were put up to provide the standard of hospitality and accommodation that visitors expected. Local and sporting events were laid on. Some holidaymakers brought sports gear with them and expected to be able to practise their chosen pastimes, which led to the first 9-hole golf course being formed at Lamlash in 1889. Mr James Allan, formerly of Balnacoole, leased Blairmore Farm and agreed to sublet part of the arable land to form the golf course.

Lamlash was considered to be the leading village then, with a branch of one of the Scottish Banks (probably the Clydesdale) located at Seafield. It had been built around 1770 on a 99 year lease from Arran Estates for the Croil family. The metal safety bars on a window were still there in the 1960s, but the site of the window has now been bricked up. There was a branch of the bank in Brodick but only open 2 days per week, whereas the Lamlash bank opened every day. The village also contained the Coastguard station, now Marine House.

The improved ferry service resulted in a huge boost to Arran's population. Incomers began to make their homes on Arran, and in 1823, the island's population reached 6500 – the highest ever recorded, before or since. The rise caused the landowners some concern. Tourism had not yet begun to be seen as a business, and they regarded the increasing numbers of new residents as a nuisance. Improved agricultural efficiency meant that fewer workers were needed, and the surplus unemployed hands were turning into a social problem the landowners did not want to deal with. Against an economic background in which a minority earned reliable money, there were far too many with no means of making a living.

The cause of this imbalance was not acknowledged, though it was obvious. In Sannox, 27 families had been evicted to create one large sheep farm extending to over 100 acres. Not unreasonably, discontent among the have-nots was rising. The more affluent tenants of relatively large farms were doing well, but for those who scraped to afford the annual rent for a few acres, little benefit was seen. If a family worked hard to improve their standard of living through better agricultural yield, the benefit was taken up by the landlord, who rewarded their efforts by increasing the rent. The annual rent review usually resulted in an increase of around five pounds a year. It was a cruelly high proportion of the barely adequate income, but if it forced the sitting family to leave their holding, the estate factor simply collected the increased rent from new occupants. It was, in effect, a steady process of discarding small tenants in favour of those able to do things on a larger scale. For the dispossessed, it started to seem that there was nothing to lose.

FIRST WROUGHT IRON PIER BUILT AT BRODICK

Leaving

There had been a gradual build-up to the realisation that life on Arran for the less favoured was becoming untenable. The weather had not helped. In the early 1800s, a series of hard winters had made it hard to survive. Even in the warmer south, there had been ice on the Thames in February 1823, and most of the country was afflicted by snow and blizzards. In 1825 the winter was one of the worst in living memory, with frequent gales causing widespread damage to crops, and there was little let-up from then on. 1828 was bitterly cold and 1829 began with hard frost, followed by a wet, cold February. 1829 was even worse, with widespread icy conditions. The Thames was frozen over from late December until the end of January.

For Arran families with no land to farm, the situation was becoming intolerable. Though people helped each other as much as they could, dispossessed families must have been acutely aware that their non-contributing presence made life even harder for relatives who shared their cramped accommodation and scanty food. Self-respecting small

REMAINS OF ONE OF THE HOUSES LEFT IN 1829, NORTH SANNOX

farmers do not take easily to the status of beggars, and the idea of leaving began to seem better than a life of embarrassing dependence. Already, many had gone.

The Rev. Alexander MacBride noted in his *New Statistical Account of Kilmory* that as early as 1821, 500 persons were 'sent away', chiefly from the Sannox district. His phrasing makes it clear that these people were not merely deprived of their traditional land but actually cleared from the islands. Some of the ejected families emigrated to North America, but by far the greater number removed to Ayrshire towns. Following this, the pressure to get rid of surplus ex-agricultural workers was stepped up. The 10th Duke, Alexander Hamilton (1767 - 1852) offered 100 acres of land to every able-bodied man over the age of 21 who was willing to go to Canada, and said he would pay 50% of the cost of the passage.

Something of a smear campaign began, describing the unwanted people of Sannox in derisory terms as so interbred that many of them were deaf and dumb. There seems no evidence of any truth in this. There was in Arran generally, as there is in all country districts, a certain amount of intermarrying, but it does not appear to have been commoner than in any other part of Scotland, nor than in English rural districts. It was certainly less common than in Norway and many other parts of the Continent. The list of surnames then in Sannox included many that were not of Arran origin and must have been those of incomers. That aside, however, the traditional Scottish names, even today, cover vast numbers of families whose blood relationship is so remote (if it exists at all) as to be immaterial.

More lasting than any such manufactured excuses has been the permanent grief and outrage felt at the expulsion of people from their homes and from the land where they belonged. Dr. Donald MacLeod, writing in 1863, expressed it perfectly when he said, 'Is not a man better than sheep? They who would have shed their blood like water for Queen and country are in other lands, Highland still, but expatriated for ever.'

In many ways, the emigration was Arran's loss, for the men and women who had the courage and confidence to step away into an unknown life were tenacious people of great energy. The Arran contingent, mainly from Lochranza and North Sannox, which had borne the brunt of forcible clearance, comprised 12 families totalling 86 people. The decision to leave had not been an easy one. Despite the financial help offered, the fee for the passage to Quebec or Montreal Canada was £4.00 for each passenger, though three children aged less than fifteen counted as one. In the 21st century, one must multiply that by at least a hundred to see what it meant. The investment in an unknown future was quite a hefty one - and the land on offer, they learned, was far from being prime arable fields. It was rough terrain, covered in scrub and mature forest - but they were assured that it had an ample supply of fresh water, so it would have to do.

Preparing for the voyage, people packed chests with the means of survival – farming implements, building tools, cooking utensils, clothing, bibles, a few items of furniture and of course spinning wheels and needlework essentials.

The departure date grew closer. They were to sail on the brig *Caledonia*, captained by Donald Miller who, reassuringly, was a native of Arran, but logistical problems abounded. Some of the chests were very bulky and heavy, presenting quite a problem in how to transport everything to Lamlash and load it onto the brig. Archibald McKillop from Lochranza, who had been the schoolmaster and had collected taxes for the Duke, took charge. He had been educated at Edinburgh University and evidently was a man of authority. He organised the use of horses to help his family transport their belongings over the drovers' path to Sannox , since the Boguille road over the north end of the island had not yet been built.

In Sannox, the Lochranza contingent joined the rest of the group, whose members gave them shelter until the day of departure, when a farewell service was held in Sannox Church. The building was only seven years old, having been constructed in 1822 following a visit by the Rev James Haldane of Campbeltown in 1806. He was a pioneer of the Congregational Church, the breakaway group that was the

A PAGEANT STAGED IN 1977 BY THE CHILDREN OF LAMLASH HIGH SCHOOL AT THE OPENING OF THE MEMORIAL TO THE EMIGRANTS WHO LEFT FOR CANADA IN THE EARLY 1800'S

beginning of the United Presbyterian Church of Scotland. Prior to the building of the church in Sannox, services had been held in the homes of various people residing there – but the use of the new building proved to be shorter-lived than they had expected. Now, many of the assembled worshippers were there for the last time.

The service was conducted by the Rev. Alexander McKay, who knew only too well of the suffering that had resulted from the new drive to agricultural efficiency. He was married to Janet, a sister of Duncan Macmillan, whose great-grandson would become the British Prime Minister - though all that lay in the future. Duncan was born in North Sannox and grew up at the Cock of Arran. He married Katherine Crawford and they occupied a small croft at Achaig Corrie until 1816. At that point they could not afford a steep hike in the rent and were forced to leave the island. MacMillan found employment in Ayrshire, transporting coal to the harbour, and their sons were educated in Troon. Daniel, born on Arran in 1813, developed a talent in writing and printing, and with his brother Alexander founded the Macmillan press in Cambridge. Daniel's grandson was

Harold Macmillan (1894 – 1986), who was Prime Minister of the United Kingdom from 1957 until 1963.

When the service was over, it was time to go. The brig lay at anchor in Lamlash Bay, having sailed from Greenock as the first stage in the long voyage to Canada. The carefully packed chests had been ferried out to the ship on small rowing boats and manhandled aboard.

A lone piper played a lament, and the Rev. Alexander McKay held a final service on the deck. He read an appropriate passage 1st Peter, chapter 5 verse 7, in both the English and Gaelic tongue, which was still the most commonly spoken language despite efforts to stamp it out. 'Casting all your care upon him: for he careth for you.'

In such trust, they left on April 25th 1829, for an unknown future.

SANNOX COTTAGE

The Voyage

The 12 families on the voyage to Canada had names that will be familiar to Arran people to this day. Archibald McKillop, who had taken charge so firmly of getting everyone to Sannox, was head of a big tribe. He brought his own family of seven, but there were more with the same surname. Donald McKillop brought eight people, Archibald McKillop, a tanner, came with nine family members and Neil McKillop, a cooper, brought eight.

Then there were the Kelsos. Robert Kelso brought six people, Alexander Kelso brought five, William Kelso had four. These big family groups apart, there was John McKinnon and his family of four, then Neil Macmillan with six. Margaret Macmillan, a cousin of Duncan Macmillan, was a widow, but embarked on the brig with four other family members. Angus Brodie, a mason and sawyer, brought six others, and Dugald McKenzie came with three. There were also four unmarried men who also had familiar Arran names. They were Robert Stewart, Donald Stewart, a sawyer, William Hendry, a carpenter and John Cook. The eldest passenger was Neil Walker, the 80-year-old father of Mrs Brodie. The youngest was William Kelso, who was born during the voyage.

The 'Caledonia' was a two masted sailing ship of 196 tons. She had a copper lined bottom and was a proven and extremely seaworthy vessel, and had made the trip to the Americas on several occasions before. This was just as well, for within a couple of days of leaving Lamlash Bay the ship encountered a violent storm off the Irish coast. Such was the ferocity of the gale that all the 180 persons on board – including experienced fishermen – were seasick. Despite the storm, the vessel suffered no great damage Shortly afterwards a stowaway from Paisley was found hiding aboard. The passengers took pity on him and raised the cost of his fare.

It could have been worse. By 1829, there was nothing particularly new about shiploads of emigrants crossing to the New World. The first sailing from Scottish shores had been in 1772, when the *Alexander* crossed the Atlantic with 201 settlers, mainly from South Uist and the mainland. Bound for St. John (now Prince Edward Island), they had all been Jacobites, and were sponsored by the Laird of Glenaladale. The following year the Dutch-built *Hector*, captained by John Spears, sailed from Greenock with 3 families and 5 single men. Once clear of the Clyde, the *Hector* headed north to Loch Broom and picked up another 33 families and 25 single men, making a total of two hundred passengers. They had a terrible time. The voyage to Pictou in Nova Scotia took almost eleven weeks, and it was surprising that the badly-found ship completed the trip. Below the waterline the conditions of the timbers were not too bad, but her superstructure was extremely poor. Most of the handrails were seriously rotten, and the below-deck accommodation was infested with rats. A quarter of the passengers, many of them children, died from smallpox or scurvy during the passage, due to lack of fresh vegetables and the unhealthy conditions.

Later emigration turned into a profitable business of transporting people to Canada on the outward journey and valuable timber on return. Some ships had a splendid record, notably the Irish *Jeanie Johnston*, built in Quebec in 1848 by the Scottish-born shipbuilder John Munn. In seven years of transporting refugees from the potato famine, she made sixteen voyages to North America, carrying as many as 254 passengers, without a single fatality. This was due to her enlightened captain, James Attridge, and a devoted qualified doctor, Richard Blennerhassel. In many other cases, the passengers were regarded as no more than cargo, unlamented if they died. For hard-hearted ship owners, deaths during the voyage saved on the overall cost of provisions and made for a higher profit margin.

In the worst cases, three out of every twenty emigrants died during the passage from illness or accidents. 830 passengers on the brig *Hercules* set out in 1853 from Campbeltown on a seven-month voyage to Australia, and 56 of them died.

Compared with that, the brig *Caledonia* had a good record. She was a well-built and reliable ship, and nobody in the Arran group died on the crossing to Canada. Sea-sickness became less of a problem as the passengers became used to the motion of the ship. The storm at the outset of the voyage meant they were a week behind schedule when they came in sight of the new promised land, but such delays were not unusual. Sailing vessels could only make such speed as the wind permitted. After weeks of gazing at an empty horizon, the immigrants were probably too excited by the sight of land on the horizon to mind a little tardiness. After travelling down the St Lawrence seaway, they arrived at Quebec on Thursday 25th June. The whitewashed cottages that had been built by the riverside raised eager hopes that something similar awaited them at the end of their journey. It was as well, perhaps, that none of them knew what lay ahead.

In fact, neither the Arran people nor the Canadians seemed to know anything. It was as if the shipload of people had arrived as a complete surprise. No arrangements had been made for them. The captain needed to begin his return journey, but was reluctant to abandon his Scottish passengers until he knew that some plan was in place. They seemed becalmed in every sense. Quebec showed no sign of either activity or wind, and after two stalled days when no information was forthcoming, Captain Miller decided to put his ship on tow and head downstream to Montreal. There, he would have to unload his human cargo, whether or not anyone knew what to do with them. When they reached Montreal, he put the travellers and their bulky luggage ashore at Point St Charles. They made a temporary camp as best they could and watched the *Caledonia*, their last link with Scotland, sail away.

Now there was nothing to do but to wash clothes, feed children and await the arrival of Mr Buchanan, the Quebec immigration agent, whose job it was to allocate their promised land in McNab township, Renfrew County, Ontario. They knew nothing about the proposed area except that it was on the Ottawa River, south west of Montreal, in an area known as Upper Canada. It had first been colonised in May 1824, five years previously, so there was some hope of meeting established settlers.

When Mr Buchanan eventually turned up he painted a discouraging picture of the McNab township. He described it as an unhealthy place, subject to logging accidents and constant fevers, and strongly advised the Arran immigrants that they would be much better to head for Megantic County in Lower Canada. Though the newcomers did not know it, Buchanan's real motive was to settle a new community in a completely undeveloped part of Quebec, but no hint of this was given.

With good common sense, the Arran folk agreed that accepting Buchanan's word about the suitability of the land would be rash. A deputation had better go and look at the suggested area, and report back. Alexander McKillop the natural leader of the group, hired a local boat to take Buchanan and four of the immigrants, including himself, back up the river to the suggested area, which was on the opposite side of the seaway from Quebec. Disembarking at the township of St.Nicholas, they hired horses and set off on a 45-mile journey inland, in an easterly direction from the river. They rode over rough terrain where there were no tracks, and the journey took them two days.

They arrived at Lac Joseph on the Becancour River. Its nearest settlement was a district named Inverness, where there was a small community of mostly Irish people, but even that was fairly remote. However, the Arran men liked what they saw. The condition of the soil was good and the surrounding area held moments of beauty, when a view could be glimpsed through the thick forest. The place had great appeal. In many ways it was similar to the mountain landscape the Arran people were used to, and in the warmth of high summer, everything was at its best. There was an abundant supply of fresh water and fish swam in the streams leading into the lake. There was no habitation of any kind - nothing but trees and water - but the ground seemed fertile. It would have to do.

Time was running on too fast for the luxury of picking and choosing. They had expected to arrive in mid-summer and get settled while the weather was still good, but with the ship's late arrival and then the delay caused by waiting for the agent, precious weeks had slipped by. The best of the summer had already gone, and there was not much time to build some kind of shelter before winter came.

They rode back to Montreal and reported their findings to

the rest of the group. Everyone agreed that there was no time to look elsewhere. They had to start building shelter for themselves, before the winter came. So they accepted Buchanan's proposal and hired a barge to take them on the return trip upriver to St Nicholas, with all their possessions. There, they engaged French Canadian teamsters to transport their possessions, together with anyone old or infirm. All the able-bodied people walked the 45 miles of rough terrain to the lake. It took them almost a week. By the time they arrived at the clearing by the lakeside, it was nearly August. They had now been in Canada for the best part of four weeks.

Once again, the Quebec agent kept them waiting. He did not arrive until late September to allocate the grant lands. The angry settlers were again marooned in a state of frustration, knowing they could not start to build even makeshift homes until they'd been told which areas were theirs. They improvised tents by stretching blankets over tree branches and pegging them down, and were lucky that the shortening autumn days were still warm.

The land agent may have delayed his journey to Lac Joseph because he knew a second group of Scottish settlers was expected. With the distances involved, he could well have decided to deal with all of the incomers in a single visit rather than settle the first contingent then have to return. The Arran families who came on the *Caledonia* were followed two months later by a group on the brig *Albion*, captained by William Hall. They had left Brodick on the steamer *Helensburgh*, which had begun a mail service in 1825, and joined the *Albion* in Greenock. It left on June 5th carrying 202 passengers and arrived in Quebec on July 24th.

A week later, they had joined the first group at Lac Joseph, increasing the size of the tented village to 109

persons from Arran. The four families that now arrived were strongly connected with the original group. There was the widowed Mrs J.McKillop and nine family members, and James Fullerton, a blacksmith, with four others, together with another widow, Mrs P. Gordon, with two relatives, and John McKenzie with four. One more family, comprising eight people and headed by Peter Sillers, a tanner and shoemaker, arrived in mid-August from the brig *Foundling,* captained by G.McLeod. That brought the total group encamped by Lac Joseph to a total of 117 men, women and children.

They were part of a vast exodus. In that single year of 1829, no fewer than 254 ships sailed from Scotland to Quebec, and a total of 5,689 Scottish settlers crossed the Atlantic ocean to start a new life. Later, an Inverness local paper reported the astonishing fact that over the years, 3,463,292 emigrants had left Scotland for Canada, America or Australia. That statistic speaks volumes about the number of people whose way of life crumbled as a result of the new and more intensive agriculture. And it is hardly surprising that today, over 4 million Canadians claim Scottish heritage.

When the land agent at last arrived, the settlers realised that the best areas of prime land by the lakeside had already been sold to speculators from Quebec. There was nothing they could do about that. More infuriating was that the agent reneged on the Duke of Hamilton's promise that every able-bodied man would receive 100 acres. Instead he allocated 100 acres to each family group, which was a very different thing. Archibald McKillop, the leader of the group, was granted 200 acres and choice of location for his numerous family members, but the others had to accept the land they were given. Some ended up in a poor situation, allocated a patch of thick forest that was some distance from the lake. One of the immigrants wrote, 'This country has much hardship, though people arriving were unaware of the truth. The evil being brought upon us through enticement and false promises by the benefactors to encourage us to emigrate.' But it was too late for recrimination. As the weather turned colder, the main problem was going to be finding a way to stay alive.

Rescue

In that crisis, the people who came to the rescue of the settlers were the Abenaki Indians. Arran people had been told that there was a settlement of incomers about two days' walk away where sixty people were reputed to live, but the only humans they saw were the cautious, brown-skinned men who watched them with perplexity from between the trees. The settlers had been told that Abenaki Indians had a camp at the head of the lake, but would have had no idea that they could get to know them.

It is difficult to imagine how communication began. The Indian people had no good reason to befriend white men, whose arrival had brought disease and warfare, but they evidently felt concerned as they saw how little the new settlers and their families knew about how to cope with this unknown terrain. The two nationalities had no language in common, but slowly they came together in the shared human skills of survival. The Abenaki showed the Scots how to use bark from the trees to build temporary shelters.

They taught the men to trap game and showed them which berries were good to eat. They made them aware of the animals that lived in the forest, some to be hunted and some to be avoided. It was a richness that included moose, deer, black bears, beavers, chipmunks, rabbits, squirrels, foxes, racoons, opossums, and skunks. There were also groundhogs and porcupines, weasels, shrews and mink. Bats flitted through the sky at evening, and there were countless varieties of birds and reptiles.

The conditions in that first winter were awful. The snow and ice lasted for months and were much harsher than anyone had experienced in Scotland. Two men lost their toes through frostbite. Another went missing during a snowstorm and was found lying dead, frozen by the path a short distance from the settlement. The snow was often many feet in depth and the metal containers used to store drinking water in the shelters where the people slept often burst when they froze solid. People would wake to find their bedclothes stiff with frost, and scraps of food left overnight would have frozen to the surface of a roughly-made table.

There had not been time to do more than make a start on building log cabins, though the men had toiled from first light to dusk, felling trees and splitting them lengthways, two men working on a long blade in a sawpit they had dug. The Indians saved the little community from disaster by showing the men how to construct tree bark shelters, and there were surprisingly few casualties. The elderly were the most vulnerable to cold, and 80 year old Neil Walker died, as did one of the widowed ladies. An outbreak of fever in the

EXAMPLE OF THE TYPE OF SHELTER THE ABENAKI SHOWED THE ARRAN SETTLERS HOW TO BUILD IN THE FIRST WINTER

first months had killed two children, Margaret Kelso, who was fifteen, and two-year-old Jane MacKillop. The rest survived, though the women often only had a meagre supply of fish, potato and milk to feed the many hungry mouths.

The Arran men and women had a broad spread of skills and talents between them, and as most of them had been small farmers as well as tradesmen, they were well used to improvising whatever was needed. They were more fortunate than some of the new settlers, since their background of sheep rearing on Arran meant they had brought good woollen clothing with them, which helped to ward off the extreme cold. Once through that first winter, the group began to raise sheep and the women were able with their spinning wheels to provide new clothing for the community.

The Arran settlers were people with the confidence to accept the challenge of emigration and the intelligence to understand that they would have to face a totally unfamiliar situation. It is obvious that few people living today would have the practicality, stamina and sheer physical strength to survive a Canadian winter with no form of support except tree-bark shelters and their own determination. Within a remarkably short time, the Arran group had mastered that basic challenge and went on to establish working practices and education for their children, together with a ministry that cared for the needs of both body and spirit.

Their first log cabins were approximately 18 feet square, divided into sections as the old Arran blackhouses had been, with partitions constructed from tree bark. The floors were made from logs split in half with the flat surface uppermost, and the walls were of whole logs, notched at the corners to provide a strong but simple joint. Inevitably, the logs were not smoothly cylindrical and there were gaps between them, but these were filled with a mixture of clay and moss to keep wind and rain out. Openings were left for a door and for windows to admit light, and in the absence of glass, timber shutters were constructed. Inevitably, these were far from draught-proof, and the cold and wind found their way in. The roof was made with cross-rafters clad with bark, and had a circular gap left to allow smoke to escape. Clay-plastered wicker was used at first to form a chimney, but the cabins were often full of smoke. There was no such thing as an enclosed stove, so for heat and cooking, an open fire had to be lit on an area of flagstones. Condition in the resulting smoke were often unbearable. Realising this, the men dug out a cellar under the next cabins they built, and this gave people a refuge from both smoke and wind, though there was no form of heat.

Open fires in dwellings built of wood and roofed with bark of course meant there was a constant danger of catching light, and there were some catastrophes. James Fullerton, the blacksmith who sailed on the *Albion,* lost his home when a spark from his forge set fire to the wooden building, and after that the settlers formed chimneys of stone.

The spring of 1830 must have come as a relief. When the snow melted and conditions improved, it gave the settlers new heart and they set about building byres and stables as well as better houses. The task of clearing ground was urgent, so that they could raise crops and keep livestock. There was no respite, and no question of any entertainment apart from perhaps the songs tucked away in memory. When the sun went down, there was nothing to do but go to bed. Unsurprisingly, the birth rate was high, but this was all to the good. As children grew, they could be useful, and the settlers needed as many hands as could be found or created.

The little community kept on growing. Letters must have been finding their way to and fro, for there was a move within the leading families to consolidate in Canada. Another group of McKillops came over on the *George Canning* in 1831, with Dugald Campbell and his family of five, plus nine people from the Kerr family. Duncan McKelvie, sawyer, came with ten others, including Donald Nichol, Archibald Cook, William McKenzie, James Stewart, who was a tailor, John Kelso and John McKinnon, all of them with families and all of them with names familiar on Arran to this day. A Mr Donald Hendry arrived in 1831 and became the settlement minister. He was a Congregationalist, as the Sannox church had been, Calvinistic in his doctrine. His sermons were delivered in Gaelic, and he could teach the language, but according to Robert McLellan's book on Arran, the Government of the new Union would not allow payment for this, as the policy was to let Gaelic die out.

The Lac Joseph community reached its maximum with that third arrival. The Arran immigrants totalled 275, having been joined by people from the island's south end as well as more from Lochranza and North Sannox The Scottish contingent brought the population of incomers in the Inverness area to 840 persons. Records in the year of 1902 show this to be the height of the Scottish settlers from Arran in Megantic County.

Those first pioneers explored more territory, and founded townships with the wide-ranging names of Inverness, Leeds, Ireland, St Agatae, Lysander falls, Rectory Hill, Wilson's Mills, St Jacques De-Leeds, Kinner's Mills, Lipsey's Hill, St Jean De-Brebeuf, and Thetford Mines.

The first half decade was a period of unrelenting hard work, but by 1834, every family had cleared parts of their allotted ground, built log cabins and barn accommodation for the livestock and created workshops cabins for men to continue their trades as carpenters, blacksmiths etc. They had put up a school for the young and the largest building, called 'the old log meeting house' was their first place of worship, with an extension at the rear to accommodate the minister and his wife. The majority of the congregation, who were regular attendees, walked to the church, and some had to cover a distance of 7 miles. Often the younger generation, dressed in their Sunday best, would walk barefoot, only putting their socks and shoes on when approaching the church. Presentable footwear was too precious to be subjected to miles of rough terrain - it was kept clean so as to be respectable for the most important occasions.

Conditions were hard; the Inverness area had virtually no roads, only rough paths through the forest. Supplies had to be brought in from St.Nicholas or Quebec from time to time, but it meant a journey on foot of 45 miles each way, stumbling over tree roots and navigating by sun or starlight across high areas of open scrubland to avoid river flooding. It was not until 1835, six years later, that roads started to be built, and it took a decade before a road system linked the settlement to St Francis, St Nicholas and Quebec.

No horses or oxen were available in those first years and everyone, both men and women, had to carry heavy loads, often with nothing but dried boiled potato to give them some sustenance. There would be a joint winter expedition by a number of the group, carrying pork, home made flour, hides, poultry and fish to trade in the market. On the return journey they would be laden with household goods - crockery, groceries, maple sugar, butter and cheese. Clothing had to be bought, too, and slates and schoolbooks for the children, together with such essentials as calico, hardware, seedlings for the gardens and medicines.

The long journey could be hazardous. On one occasion the returning men found the river in spate. They were confronted by a torrent of floodwater, and there was no choice but to wade through it, up to their chests in the fast-moving river, with the 56lb bags balanced on their heads to keep the flour dry. In mid-winter, on a New Year's day, Dugald McKenzie, who had come over with the second group on the *George Canning,* set out to get flour for his family, and he, too, had to ford the flooded river. He stripped his clothes off in order to keep them dry, but although the crossing was short he became so chilled that it was difficult to put his clothes back on, and he ran for a distance to generate some heat in his body. On returning with the half-hundredweight of flour, he knew fording the river was impossible, and walked upstream until he came to a place where the water was frozen solid enough to bear his weight.

The women, too, were capable of extraordinary strength and endurance. One of them carried a bushel of wheat to the mill eleven miles away, waited until it had been ground and carried it back on the same day. They went through pregnancy and childbirth with very little help or let up in the work, and with no medical aid apart from the 'old wives' traditional remedies and the herbal knowledge of their Indian advisor, Peter Mountain.

Their strength and stamina were phenomenal. But it is doubtful whether they could have survived as they did without the help of the Indians.

The Abenaki and their country

The Abenaki, whose name meant 'people of the east' came originally from the Appalachian mountain range that once joined the big land-masses of the northern world, linking with the Caledonian chain that still outcrops in Scotland and Scandinavia . 'Abenaki' was a group name that encompassed many tribes living in Northern New England and Southern Quebec, including Pennacook, Winnipesaukee, Pigwacket, Cowasuck, Penobscot and Wawenock. They had lived in these traditional lands for as much as ten thousand years, and numbered between forty and fifty thousand people. They belonged to the large Algonquin language family, speaking a tongue that would be understood in much of New England, New Hampshire, Vermont, Maine and New Brunswick.

When Europeans first landed in the Americas in the early 1500s, the effect on the native Indians was disastrous, for they had no immunity against the diseases brought in by the new settlers. Epidemics decimated their numbers, the worst one being between 1564 and 1570, followed by typhus

in 1586. Barely thirty years later, between 1610 and 1620, three separate epidemics swept through New England and the Canadian Maritimes. Maine was particularly hit hard in 1617, where smallpox killed 75% of the Indian population. Influenza, diphtheria, measles and chicken pox continued to take an unstoppable toll. By 1783, after the American Revolution, the total Abenaki population was little more than a thousand. In less than 150 years, a people who had numbered nearly 50,000 had been reduced to little more than a handful.

In view of this tragedy, it is astonishing that the Abenaki living near Lac Joseph were so helpful to the immigrants from Arran. Clearly, they felt compassion for these helpless people who were trying so hard to find some way to live in this unknown place. Perhaps some natural immunity to disease was now protecting the survivors of the many plagues, for certainly, the Scottish people and the Indians found ways to live together and help each other. The Scots were good at tool-making and spinning, and showed the Indians how to build more effective ploughs, but the Indians taught the Arran people an understanding of their new land and how to use it. Mutual respect blossomed. Peter Mountain, renowned for his knowledge as a herbalist and as a musician, became the Scottish families' physician and was held in great esteem. When he died, he was buried in the Boutelle cemetery on the Dublin Road, Inverness, as a mark of the respect the settlers had for him.

Those in authority had less respect. Just as in the Scottish Clearances, there was no recognition that the traditional ways of aboriginal people could be valuable. The incoming Europeans took possession of the Indians' land, and in 1676 further disruption was caused by the King Philip War that raged in that year between colonists and the native Americans. There was no doubt about who was going to win. By 1880 the Abenaki were forced to abandon their remaining lands, due to the development of forestry and mining. It was to their misfortune that the Appalachian mountain range was found to be rich in mineral deposits.

Abénaki d'Odanak

There is now a population of about 15,000 Abenaki in the whole of Canada and the United States of America, including what remains of the Algonquin people from New England, who had joined with the Abenaki as refugees in the war. All of them live on reservations.

The Abenaki, left to themselves, understood very well how to survive and prosper in their traditional landscape. They located their villages close to navigable rivers, where the adjacent floodplains were suitable for raising crops, and though they were effective hunters and fishermen, they were skilled farmers. Some of their cultivated areas extended to as much as 250 acres. They made canoes from tree bark and used fish, not only as food but where there was a surplus, as a fertiliser that increased the yield of corn. As the Arran people had done before the run-rig system was ended, they farmed communally, sharing their crops of maize, beans, corn and squash between them. The ancient hunter-gatherer way of life still underpinned their survival system, and they relied heavily on hunting, trapping, fishing and gathering nuts and berries. They were nomadic to some extent, moving their lodges further inland during the winter to follow the herds of game and returning to their riverside villages in the spring. Sometimes they would construct an oval-shaped long house, but mostly they preferred the smaller, dome shaped bark wigwams.

The first colonists took over the Indian lands in Quebec and many other places for themselves, without any form of compensation. The dispossessed Indians then had to turn a hand to any work they could find, and they were relentlessly harried. The film, *North West Passage*, from a book written by Kenneth Roberts in 1937, tells the story of how the Abenaki encampment near St Francis in Quebec was routed by the Rangers, an independent company commanded by Major Robert Rogers and attached to the British army. Rogers trained his men in the Indian skills of survival and fighting, using Indian guides who came from tribes that were the traditional enemies of the Abenaki.

Famille abénakise d'Odanak

People then and now

Many of the family names that figure in the Megantic narrative still have an active presence on Arran. A single surname may of course cover an immense number of people, since the old clans that developed in a particular area or island split and extended as people became more mobile. By the 18th century, there had already been a shift away from specific areas dominated by the ruling clan. It was replaced by a mixture of people who had arrived in whatever place offered good land and a potential living. In our own time, Scots are scattered all over the world, partly due to the Clearances but also through the curiosity and enterprise that have always been such a strong Scottish characteristic.

Despite that, there is a sense of continuum in recognising the names in this story as familiar today on Arran. Some families removed themselves so completely that their names do not appear in a current telephone directory, but others are still working on the island. Since records have become easier to access, a strong interest in genealogy has developed, and perhaps a new feeling of how real the people were who left Sannox and Lochranza in those desperate days of dispossession.

Some names have a natural prominence. James Fullerton, the blacksmith whose house burned down, had a son also called James who left the lakeside to work in the lumber trade near Quebec. Oxen were used to haul the felled trees, and for this heavy work they needed to be shod as horses are. One day the farrier who normally performed this service fell sick, but someone told the contractor that James was a handy blacksmith, taught by his father. Young James did so well that he was offered a permanent job, paid at a much higher rate than lumberjacking had done. That winter he sent home a useful sum for the benefit of his parents.

The McKillop family was - and still is - an outstanding group of talented people. Archibald, the group leader, supervised the new settlement beside Lac Joseph and over a period of eight years, saw it established as a stable, thriving community. However, in 1837 the Lower Canada Rebellion, also known as the Patriots' War, broke out. This was a conflict between the British colonial power and the rebels of Lower Canada, and Archibald had no hesitation about backing the new holders of power. He went to Quebec and volunteered for service, and was accepted at once. He quickly became the Captain of a company that he established through his own efforts, and by the end of the rebellion he had been promoted to the rank of Colonel. The victory over the rebels was absolute. During the two-year conflict, 32 men of the colonial force were killed and 47 were wounded, whereas the Patriots lost 73 men, and 1,600 were wounded. Following the end of the war, 29 men were executed for treason and 58 were deported to Australia

Archibald's son, Archie junior, became an equally distinguished man, though through more peaceful means. Born in Lochranza on July 4th 1824, he had been five years old when his family came to Canada, and from an early age, he showed promise in writing. His father, himself a university graduate, was well aware of the importance of a good education, so he gave the boy every encouragement.

REVEREND RONALD MCKILLOP AND HIS FAMILY,

DESCENDANTS OF THE FIRST COLONISTS, CIRCA 1888

A SCOTTISH COUPLE
(CELTIC ROUTE COLLECTION)

From the local school in the Inverness area, young Archie was sent to study at Lachine in Quebec, then completed his studies at Toronto University. From there, he quickly became known as a charismatic and controversial public speaker. He came back often to his parents' home by Lac Joseph, but one of these visits led to disaster.

On a Christmas vacation when Archie was helping on the farm, he was accidentally kicked in the head by an ox. This damaged his sight, and within two years he was totally blind. However, it did not stop him from pursuing his vocation. He continued to write poetry, and became known as the Blind Bard, in demand all over the province as a speaker. He was devoted to the Temperance cause and was never afraid to express his opinions. A challenging, controversial individual in the political and religious world, he was an honest person with a great love for children. Like many of the famous poets who preceded him, he had a passion for the outdoors and the natural world, which was reflected in many of his poems. He also had a great loyalty to his Scottish ancestry. The Scottish Society of Canada recognised him as their bard and many years after his blindness, invited him to speak to them as their guest of honour.

CELTIC POET & BARD ARCHIBALD MCKILLOP

Archie died in September 1905 in Kingston Ontario. His body was brought back to Lac Joseph, to what had become known as the 'Arran Scots Settlement Camp' and buried beside the grave of his father in the Congregational Chapel Cemetery. His name lives on.

Others whose last resting-place is in the country that became their new home should perhaps be listed as well, for each one of them contributed to the making of a new life. Each was born on Arran but died in Canada.

In Boutelles Cemetery, by the Dublin Road, there are the following members of the McKillop family:

Mary McKillop 1824 – 1910, Mary McKenzie McKillop 1792 - 1875, John McKillop 1783 -1859, Cathrine McKillop 1825 - 1915, AlexanderMcKillop 1827 - 1910.

In Adderley Presbyterian Cemetery, by Gosford Road, are the following:

John D McKenzie 1826 - 1874 and his wife,

Marion Brodie 1829 -1908, James

McKenzie 1870 -1877, Mary McKenzie

1857 - 1874, John McKinnon 1832 - 1900,

John McKinnon 1803 - 1898.

The Congregational Chapel cemetery, by Hamilton Road, has some graves where the dates are incomplete. It includes the following:

Rev Donald Hendry 1774 -1847, Elizabeth Kelso, wife of Angus Brodie, 1881, Isabella, wife of Archibald McKillop, Cathrine McKillop 1806 - 1888, John McKillop 1800 -1878, John McKillop 1871, Mary McKillop 1770 - 1842, Neil McKillop 1767 -1858, Peter McKillop 1864, Donald Sillars 1894, John Sillars 1859, Archibald McKillop (The Blind Bard)

1825 - 1904.

The following is one of Archie McKillop's poems, composed in 1872 when he was 48 years old. It stands as the perfect epitaph, both for himself and so many others, illuminated by a real love of the place which became their new home.

Megantic More Than Forty Years Ago

Old Megantic banks and braes, lovely lakes and balmy bowers,

Where in childhood's happy days we have culled the fairest flowers,

See that mountain's towering head, see this vale so green and low,

Mountains rise and valleys spread, just as forty years ago.

Here the silvery streamlets pour, down the dewy dell at morn,

There the mountains' torrents roar laughs the Ioudest laugh to scorn,

Here when young I loved to roam, nature's wildest charms

to know,

Here our fathers found a home, more than forty years ago.

Where the hills of Arran swell; high above Lochranza's shore,

Few there are that live to tell of the friends they saw no more

When from Scotia's favoured strand, still unstained by

conquering foe,

Sailed that hopeful hardy band, more than forty years ago.

Dark and dense the wild woods lay; gaily green for leagues around,

Here the savage beasts of prey undisturbed asylum found,

Then with pioneering toils, stalwart arms with many a blow

Felled the woods and burned the piles, more than forty

years ago.

Now the ploughman guides his steeds; where the great old woods have been,

See our gardens, orchids, meads, oh, what changes we have seen,

Ordered by unerring law, seasons come and seasons go,

Gone, the rarest sights we saw, more than forty years ago.

Gone the camps and camping ground, old log meeting

house and all,

Gone the schools assembled round, fires that blazed against

the wall,

Gone the barns and houses too, roofed with bark in many a row,
Frames and shingles known to few, more than forty years ago.

Now we build our palace piles, some of wood and some of stone,
Roofed in strange, fantastic styles, bark forgotten and unknown,
Gone the simple ways of life, early years were wont to know,
Less of law and less of strife, more than forty years ago.

Gone the fathers; they are dead, gone their kind, endearing ways,
Worn the bibles that they read, mute their earnest songs of praise,
Gone, a generation gone, all forgotten, lying low,
When most noble deeds were done, more than forty years ago.

We who live in Canada, now the new dominion styled,
Still remember when we saw Inverness a desert wild,
And Megantic all around, with parishes below,

But an Indian hunting ground, more than forty years ago.

I am older, so are you, growing older day by day,
Surely we are dying too. Ah! How soon to pass away,
But Megantic shall remain, mountains rise and rivers flow,
Who shall then in sweeter strain, sing of forty years ago?

And now ...

The people who went from Arran so long ago are not forgotten. The memorial to them stands in the form of three great stones in Lamlash, which seem to lean towards each other in grief for the loss of people who were in many cases forced from their land. They are carefully chosen stones, brought from a quarry near Balachulish. Builder John Thomson constructed the base and Arran Transport was engaged to transport the stones. The drivers were E.I.Cannon of Lamlash and Phil Currie of Whiting Bay. Mrs Myrtle Cook Maxwell of New Brunswick, Canada, unveiled the memorial in Lamlash, during a service and ceremony held on May 9th 1977.

Family connections with the Megantic settlers continue. As far as can be ascertained, none of the original settlers came back to Arran - which was hardly surprising. Building a new life out of native forest was a challenging task, and no interested sponsor would subsidise a six-week sea trip for an emigrant who fancied a trip home. However, the notable McKillop family, so prominent in this story of the group who

Erected on behalf of
Arran clearance descendents across North America
to their brave forefathers
who departed from their beloved island home to Canada
during the clearance years 1829 to 1840
Here at Lamlash on April 25th 1829
part of the clearance (86 souls)
when embarking on the brig Caledonia (196 tons)
the Rev. A. Mackay preached from The Mound (opposite)
formed by the departing
his text "Casting all your care upon him: for he careth for you."
1st Peter ch.5 v.7
The Caledonia arrived at Quebec City June 25th 1829
The group was the first of more than 300 Arran colonists
of Megantic County, Province of Quebec
The largest group, more than 400, had as their destination
the seaport town of Dalhousie, New Brunswick
to be pioneer settlers of
the Restigouche-Bay Chaleur District
"Yet still the blood is strong, the heart is highland."
A chlann eilean mo ghaoil bithibh dìleas d'a chéile

went out in 1829, continues, and there are descendants living and working on Arran to this day.

Robert Watt, the renowned folk singer, lives in Quebec but is related to the original Arran settlers. His album called *Homeland* contains a very moving spoken explanation of how and why the Arran settlers came to Megantic County, coupled with the haunting Scottish songs they brought with them. He includes, too, music from their new land, notably an Indian song with a drumbeat accompaniment called *Buffalo Jump.*

Looking to the future, there is a well-established plan to rebuild the Sannox Congregational Church where a service for the emigrants leaving the clachan was held in 1829. When that happens, it will be celebrated by a visit from, hopefully, a large group from Megantic County. The advent of the Internet has put a modern finger on old history, making it newly possible for people who did not know of each other's existence to get in touch. The Atlantic Ocean no longer takes six weeks to cross. Facilities such as Skype

SANNOX CHURCH & MANSE, THE EMIGRANTS FROM NORTH SANNOX BUILT A COPY OF THIS CHURCH IN CANADA . IT WAS DESTROYED BY FIRE IN THE LATE 1800'S

enable people to see each other as well as talk, and e-mails are untroubled by weather or time.

Descendants of families who stayed are rediscovering those who went, and vice versa. People begin to know each other anew, regardless of location. When the plan to recreate Sannox church is made real, there will be a full circle. What seemed to be an end becomes a new beginning.

Though so many of the McKillop family emigrated, at least one branch stayed in North Glen Sannox, working as fishermen and later as boat builders and joiners. More recently, descendants of other branches who had settled on the mainland have answered the call of Arran and returned, bringing back a new generation. The Arran connection with its old families lives on. Let us hope it always will.

MRS MYRTLE COOK MAXWELL OF NEW BRUNSWICK, CANADA, UNVEILING THE MEMORIAL MAY 9TH 1977

THE ARRAN MCKILLOP FAMILY TREE

Archibald McKillop = Catherine McMillan
(1760-1817) (1786-1817)

Archibald McKillop = Jessie McKay
(1817-1887) (1817-1900)

Alexander McKay McKillop = Elizabeth Johnson Brown
(1857-1919) (1863-1939)

Alexander McKillop = Isabel McArthur Houston
(1904-2004) (1905-1978)

Alexandra Kathleen McKillop = Gordon MacVicar
(b 1947) (1943-1988)

Lynne Kathleen MacVicar
(b 1976)

Boat built by Alexander & Archibald McKillop, Joiners, Undertakers & Boatbuilders, Gowanlea Sannox 1877 -1819, pictured at the Arran Heitage Museum

GOWANLEA (LEFT) & LHAIMRIG, SANNOX,ISLE OF ARRAN

Bibliography and acknowledgements

Annals of Megantic County, published by Dugald McKenzie McKillop in 1902. (Dugald was the son of Donald McKillop, who died in 1895, and Donald was the son of Neil McKillop who left Sannox in 1829.)

Arran Journal by John Burrell. This large-sized, facsimile edition of Burrell's diaries, volumes 1 and 2, was published by Lady Jean Fforde.

The Story of Arran by Robert McLellan, David and Charles 1970

New Statistical Account of Kilmory by Rev Alexander MacBride

Alan J.S. Paterson Clyde steamers 1864- 1914 (2 editions printed in 1969 and 1972)

The Celtic Way 324 Chemin, Gosford, Sud Inverness, Qc G0S 1K0, Canada

History of the Highland and Agriculture Society 1880

Tour of Scotland and Voyage in the Hebrides 1775 by Thomas Pennant (1726-1798

The author would like to thank all the people who have helped in the research for this book. Robert Watt, Kate Hartley, Sandra Kerr and Lynn McVicar, as surviving members of the emigrant families, offered valuable advice, as did Grace Small of the Arran Heritage Museum. Margaret Wright unearthed a wealth of detail on the genealogy of the Megantic settlers and Heather Gough provided a capable pair of hands as proof-reader.

Edited by Alison Prince.

Design, type-setting and production by Margo Wheeler.